Monkey Stuff

Rebecca Bielawski

www.booksbeck.com

©2011 Rebecca Bielawski
Monkey Stuff by Rebecca Bielawski is licensed under the
Creative Commons Attribution-NonCommercial-NoDerivs 3.0
Unported License. To view a copy of this license, visit
http://creativecommons.org/licenses/by-nc-nd/3.0/

MUMMY NATURE
SERIES

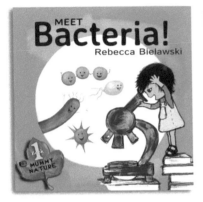

More children's books

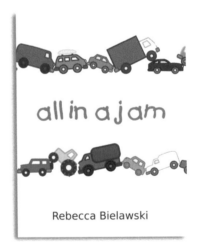

See preview pages, book planning sketches and author articles
and stay up to date on book promos and new releases by Rebecca Bielawski
Ebooks and print books in English and Spanish

www.booksbeck.com

1

There was a cow, she had one bell.
She always wore it, but then one day, well...

A little monkey,
   Brown and cheeky,

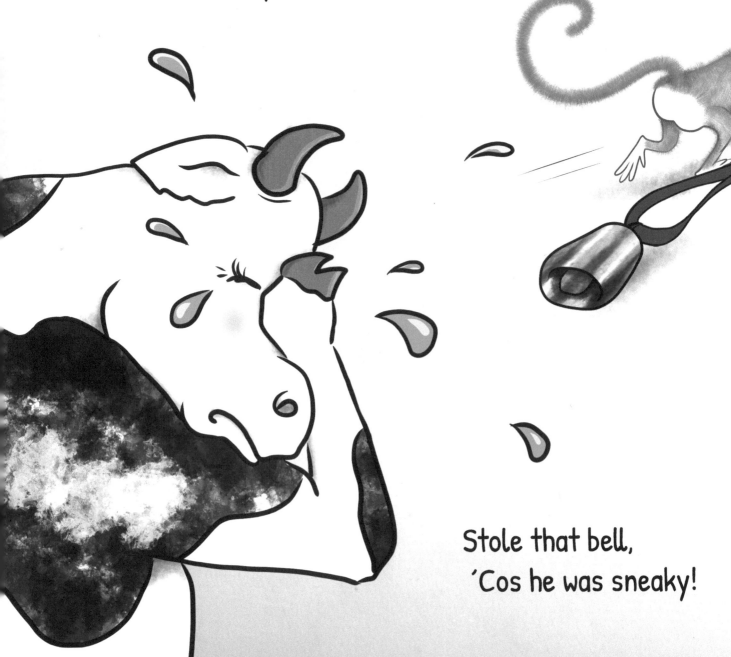

Stole that bell,
   'Cos he was sneaky!

There was a dog,
    He had two bones.
        Sometimes one buries
        What one owns.

So, he dug a hole
    In the ground

2

And buried his bones,
    That digging hound...

But that same little monkey
Came back around.

There was a bird.
Three eggs she laid.

Nearby that nest
She always stayed.

3

That rascal monkey
Snuck up one day,

Snatched those eggs
And ran away.

There was a pony
With four horseshoes.

They were items that
She could not lose.

4

Nevertheless,

One summer evening,

The monkey stole them
And danced while leaving!

There was a baker.
He baked five buns,

Those light and tasty,
Crispy ones.

The monkey appeared
And took the lot,

Then ran off juggling them...   They were hot!

There was an ant,
Six slippers she wore.

They kept her feet cosy
On the cold dirt floor.

6

The monkey took them
And didn't think.

He didn't expect
That they would stink!

There was a princess.
She wore seven pearls

To make her look better
Than the other girls.

7

8

A crocodile,
  He loved to smile.
    He had eight teeth,
      But one night while...

9

Nine apples grew
Upon a tree,

Red and crispy
And soooo juicy!

But someone came
A-swinging through,
And grabbed those apples...

Can you guess who?

Ten hairs were in
The lion's mane.

He combed them often,
- He was vain!

That pesky monkey
Was looking on.
One single snip...

And those hairs
were gone!

There was a monkey.
He had lots of stuff.

But he never seemed
To have enough.

He had:

1 cowbell,

2 bones,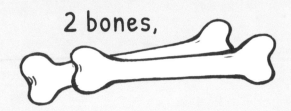

3 eggs,

4 horseshoes,

UUUU

5 buns,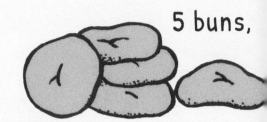

6 slippers,

7 pearls,

8 teeth,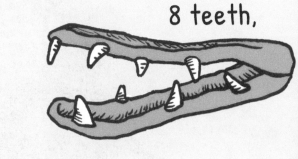

9 apples and

10 hairs.

Everyone had lost
Something of
theirs.

But the monkey felt
A bit bad inside.
Because of him,
A cow had cried.

In the end, the things were returned.

Mum said, "No stealing!"
And the lesson was learned.

CPSIA information can be obtained
at www.ICGtesting.com
Printed in the USA
LVHW071939280422
717482LV00002B/148